LEAD LIKE WATER

MANY CAN MANAGE, FEW CAN LEAD

JAMES BIRD GUESS

First Print Edition: August 2014
ISBN-13: 978-0-9897709-1-0
Printed in the United States of America

James Bird Guess International Success Academy
391 E. Las Colinas Blvd.
Suite 130-350
Irving, TX 75039
www.JamesBirdGuess.com
www.InternationalSuccessAcademy.com

For information about author appearances or bulk discounts, please visit our website, www.InternationalSuccessAcademy.com, or e-mail us at info@internationalsuccessacademy.com.

Editor: Jill Becker (www.jillbecker.net)
Cover and formatting: Streetlight Graphics (www.streetlightgraphics.com)

"Empty your mind, be formless. Shapeless, like water. If you put water into a cup, it becomes the cup. You put water into a bottle and it becomes the bottle. You put it in a teapot, it becomes the teapot. Now, water can flow or it can crash. Be water, my friend."

— **Bruce Lee**

DEDICATION

Here's to those who lead authentically
regardless of power, title, or authority.

And to those who hunger for insight to start
the process of authentic leadership.

ACKNOWLEDGMENTS

GOD!

TABLE OF CONTENTS

INTRODUCTION: LEADING LIKE WATER

In today's workplace, many can manage, but few can lead. And many organizations are deficient in authentic leaders, the type of leaders who can influence others without intimidation and motivate teams to achieve remarkable results without having to use money or rewards as a motivator.

These authentic leaders are not born, but made. Does that mean anyone can be an authentic leader? Yes! However, all of us have various degrees of potential that will distinguish the average from the good and the good from the great, but all of us have the potential to be authentic leaders. You must recognize your leadership potential and grind for it. Leadership is not an event, not a two-day seminar or a corporate retreat, not reading a best-selling book, but rather a process of growth. Growth only occurs during the process of change. And change begins with awareness, desire, and deliberate practice.

What is it that makes some leaders remarkably better than others? The most successful authentic leaders are like water. Instead of being powerful, they are essential. More than likely, you have encountered a few authentic leaders in your professional career or maybe even worked for one. Remember, they were the ones who left and other employees followed them wherever they went, even to other organizations. When they do leave prematurely, teams get dehydrated, motivation dries up and shrivels, and entire departments and organizations collapse. Just like water, they are essential. Can you name one living thing that can survive without water? And since nothing can survive without water, it's imperative that we learn from water.

Water is essential to all things, just as authentic leaders are essential to all successful organizations. Water covers more than 60 percent of the earth's surface. Water also makes up more than 60 percent of a human's body weight.

Water always flows to the lowest level. Authentic leaders are servants; they eat last, stay humble, put others first, and seek input from the lowest levels in organizations.

Water is adaptable. It has the ability to adapt to meet changing circumstances. Depending on the situation, water can be a solid, liquid, or gas. Authentic leaders are flexible and can adapt to different personality styles and workplace situations.

Water can be hard, like ice, when it needs to be.

Authentic leaders know when to be firm and direct.

Water can also be soft and gentle, like a beautiful pond. Authentic leaders understand the "hard stuff" is the "soft stuff" and they display empathy and show people they care.

Water is clear and transparent. Authentic leaders are open, upfront, and honest. They constantly make themselves vulnerable, and that is how they earn trust, because they trust others first.

Lastly, *water is persistent*. Water can cut through rock, not because of its power, but because of its persistence. Authentic leaders persevere. They know that great captains of ships are not made during calm oceans. They stay focused on the vision. Although their strategy may change, the vision remains the same until achieved.

Water is a powerful substance. And depending on how it's utilized, it can be destructive or constructive. If there is the right amount of energy surrounding it, it can cause floods or hurricanes, or it can be used to generate electricity.

The key to leading like water is to be strong but don't bully, be caring but not weak, be visionary but not impulsive, be humble but not timid, be confident but not arrogant, and be passionate but not scattered.

CHAPTER 1:
BECOMING BUTTERFLIES
BEFORE CATERPILLARS

Sometimes caterpillars try to become butterflies too fast and their wings and bodies become deformed because they didn't complete the growth process and they are never able to fly.

Cristian was recently promoted to director of the accounting department as a result of his remarkable performance, organizational skills, and ability to develop new processes. He has worked as a peer with six people on the team for the past three years. One of his team members, Ana, who has been with the company for almost ten years, also applied for the same promotion but did not get it.

Ana has now become jealous and bitter and is focused on "getting even" with upper management for promoting Cristian over her. Cristian decided not to address Ana about it directly because he felt it would be too uncomfortable. However, in meetings, Ana has started to undermine Cristian's ideas, does not share pertinent information with him on various projects, and spreads negativity to the other team members about his lack of leadership skills.

Cristian has become increasingly frustrated with Ana's behavior, and because he dislikes confrontation, has asked his other employees and former peers what he should do. His employees shared a few ideas with him, but none to Cristian's liking. Recently, Cristian e-mailed Ana requesting that she "please watch your tone with me and your other co-workers and cooperate better." Ana replied with an e-mail to the entire department saying, "I am a professional team player who is here to get results. Please be more specific with your criticism of my performance. By the way, have you developed our team's vision or are you more focused on me instead of the rest of the team?"

After many sleepless nights, Cristian attempts to terminate Ana, but after reviewing her employee file, he discovers that she is a remarkable performer who has exceeded expectations on her last three performance reviews. Feeling frustrated and at a loss for ways to deal with Ana, Cristian decides that he will do the unthinkable and finally confront her in person.

It is Friday afternoon around 4:45 p.m. and most of the department has left for the weekend. Cristian has just finished rehearsing exactly what he will say to Ana in their meeting. His palms are sweating and his heart starts to race as he walks out the door toward Ana's work area. He approaches Ana and asks to speak with her for a few minutes. Ana replies, "Let me finish my last thought in this e-mail and I'll be right with you." As she presses send, she turns around and looks Cristian directly in the eyes. Cristian, feeling pierced and not confident, looks away and says, "Let's talk in my office." Ana replies, "I'd feel more comfortable if we talked in the conference room instead, plus it's closer."

As they walk toward the conference room, Cristian is following Ana and for some reason feels powerless. He asks himself, "Am I the leader or is she?" As they walk into the conference room, Ana sits down and asks, "How can I help you?"

"We have to talk about your attitude," says Cristian.

"My attitude?" Ana replies in a strong voice.

"Yes, your attitude and arrogance, like you ..."

Ana immediately interrupts him and stands up. "Let me tell you something, buddy," she asserts. "I've been around a lot of great leaders and high performers, and honestly, you don't have what it takes. You and I both know you can't fire me because my performance speaks for itself, so you're all out of options. I suggest you act like a leader, take your paper-thin promotion and leave me alone, because I have more influence than you know."

Cristian asks desperately, "Why can't you just play nice? What did I do to you?"

Ana shakes her head and says, "You're not cut out

for this leadership stuff. This meeting is over. I have to pick up my kids."

As Ana walks out the door, she turns, smiles, and says, "Enjoy your weekend, boss!"

Cristian drops down in his chair, takes a deep breath, and begins biting his nails. As he leans back in the chair, he notices a framed picture on the wall with a motivational quote by an unknown author that reads, "Leadership is never black and white. It is always fifty shades of gray."

As the weeks turn into months, the vice president of finance, Jamie, is meeting with Cristian.

"Cristian, you've been the manager now for about six months. How do you think things are going?"

Cristian, trying hard to resist the urge to bite his nails, scratches his head and responds, "Okay, I guess. The staff likes me and I like them."

Jamie smiles as he gets up from his executive chair. "Cristian, do you think as a manager or leader that it is better to be feared, respected, or liked?"

"I think if your employees like you, they will work hard for you, so I try to get people to like me," he replies.

Jamie analyzes Cristian's statement. "So people can like you as a person but not respect you as a professional, would you agree?"

"Yes," says Cristian, although uncertain if his

response is correct.

"Cristian, does your staff think this way about you?"

Cristian pauses to think for a moment. "I don't think so. I think people know that I am really good at my job, since I make all my deadlines, get my reports completed, and so I ..."

Jamie interrupts him, saying, "That's great, and I completely agree that you do a remarkable job of managing tasks. But if we were to ask people about your performance when it comes to leading a team, which includes developing, encouraging, and growing people, what do you think they would say?"

Cristian starts bouncing his right knee feverishly and scratching the back of his head. "Jamie, honestly, it's been really tough for me. I mean, Ana . . ." Realizing he said her name, Cristian quickly backtracks, saying, "You know dealing with this one employee is like a war for me."

"Tell me more about Ana," says Jamie.

"She just has it out for me. She is so jealous that I got the job over her, and now she is trying to take my job. She's negative in meetings and since she's been here longer than me, people, you know, respect her."

Jamie is listening with his arms folded, leaning against the back window on his wall.

"I can't let her win, and right now, I'll admit she's winning," says Cristian. "She has the majority of the team against me, and they don't believe I should be in the position now because of her."

"So, what's your plan?" Jamie asks.

"Well, as you know, I've tried to discipline her because she was insubordinate and disrespectful to me, but HR said I couldn't for whatever reason," Cristian says sarcastically.

Jamie starts to walk toward Cristian, but accidentally bumps a glass of ice water on his desk, and an ice cube tumbles out and water splashes across his desk. Cristian jumps up to help, but Jamie stops him. "Just watch for a second," he instructs Cristian.

Cristian, looking confused, watches as the ice cube sits motionless and the water flows modestly and gently to the lowest level of the hard desk and then begins dripping onto the floor. Cristian, still looking confused, glances at Jamie, wondering why he is letting the water ruin his desk and floor.

"What do you see, Cristian?" asks Jamie.

"Uh, spilled water on a very expensive desk."

"Well, I see a few things. I see a hard piece of ice that tumbled onto an even harder desk and got nowhere since both objects are solid. Then I saw soft water easily flowing across the hard desk. Now I see the hard ice cube slowly melting, and as it melts it's able to go where it wants to go, which is always the lowest level."

"Wow, you see all that?" Cristian asks, but in the back of his mind he's thinking to himself that Jamie is officially crazy.

"Cristian, right now in your position as director, you are like the ice cube and Ana is like the desk. So why can't you get anywhere with her?"

"Because maybe I'm being too hard on her."

"Not necessarily on her, but with her. You are both being hard, trying to compete and defeat each other and so you both get nowhere."

"So are you saying I should let her win?" asks Cristian.

"Warm your cold heart with empathy. Embrace and encourage her. I'm not saying you will change her, because you can't change people. You can only change how you respond to people, which may change how they respond to you. That's how water gets where it wants to go over something hard. It humbles itself. Did you humble yourself with Ana, and did you even show you cared about her feelings about being passed over for the promotion?"

"No, I didn't," answers Cristian. "That's really good advice," he tells Jamie. "And I will get right on it."

"Cristian, right now people probably like you because you're a good person, but they don't respect you. And if they don't respect you, they won't follow you. And if they won't follow you, your ability to lead effectively and execute our strategic plan will be limited. Wouldn't you agree?"

Hesitantly, Cristian replies, "Yes, that's true."

"Cristian, do you know how you can earn their respect?"

"By following your advice immediately, of course."

"Well, it's going to take more than that, and I want to give you that opportunity."

"Okay, so what do you want me to do?"

"I am going to demote you back to your original position."

Cristian is surprised and confused. "How can I earn their respect as a leader if you don't give me the title and authority?"

"It's simple. You don't need a title to be a leader, because authentic leadership is about actions, not title, power, or authority. Right now, people have to follow you, and your job is to influence them to want to follow you, and that will take time. Don't be discouraged by this. We promoted you because you were good at your job and were good at managing tasks, but we failed to make sure you were equipped with the tools essential to leading people."

"But Ana will think she won. And I assume you're going to give her the position?"

"The difference between what Ana thinks and what you know should be all you need to motivate you on your journey toward good leadership. The position will remain open for the first authentic leader we recognize is ready to both manage tasks and lead people."

"So how long will it take for me to become this authentic leader and get my job back?"

"That depends on you. Just keep in mind that leadership is not an event, it's a process."

LEADERSHIP DROPS OF INSIGHT

◆　　◆　　◆

If people *fear* you, they will do what you say
Just enough to get by or receive pay
You will never get the best performance out of them

If people *like* you, they will smile and laugh
When you do things they disagree with
That feeling of like will soon pass
Like the weather, how fast your
relationships will change

If people *respect* you, they may disagree with you
Even worse, they may not like you
But despite that, you will find they
will still perform for you

◆　　◆　　◆

CHAPTER 2:
THE PROFESSIONAL
AND THE AMATEUR

*Excellence is a habit. Unfortunately,
so is mediocrity.*

Angie is a registered nurse at Taylor Medical Center. As she eats her last bite of cake at her co-worker Susan's retirement party, she thinks to herself, "That will never be me. All those years of stress and frustration and Susan has nothing to show for it. She has pretty much been in the same position her entire career."

After the final applause for Susan, people begin to leave the room and head back to work. Angie walks up to Susan and says, "Congrats on your retirement."

"Thanks," says Susan. "I am so ready to just spend time with my grandchildren after all these years being a nurse and helping people."

Angie smiles back at her.

"Hey, you got a minute?" Susan asks Angie as she

closes the door of the conference room.

"Sure. What's up?"

"You know, you remind me of me when I was your age," Susan tells her. "You have a lot of potential and I just want you to know that if you truly follow that"—Susan points to a picture on the wall that reads "EDGE," an acronym for "everyday giving excellence"—"the sky is the limit for you within this company."

"Thank you. I definitely will," says Angie in a somewhat sarcastic tone.

"Look, I know as your former manager that you and I never really got along, and that you think I was hard on you."

Angie's face goes from a smile to a frown as she folds her arms defensively. "As of today, you're not my boss anymore, but I appreciate the feedback as always," she tells Susan. "I also appreciate how you would criticize my performance in front of my peers, give me the hardest work, and ..."

Susan stops her and says, "Do you know why? Do you know why I did all those things?"

"Yeah, because you didn't want me to look good and take your job, and so you made my life a living hell. And now you expect me to sit here on the day of your retirement party and act like nothing ever happened."

Susan listens and waits. "Is that it?" she asks.

"Yes, I have nothing else to say."

"Well, let me speak my piece and then I will go." Susan goes over to a table and picks up a bottle of water and hands it to Angie.

"I'm not thirsty," says Angie, looking confused.

"That's the problem."

"What?" Angie shrugs her shoulders and wrinkles her face.

Susan then hands her another piece of cake on a plate.

"Look, I'm not hungry either."

"Again, that's your problem," says Susan.

"What are you talking about? Can you speak English, please!" Angie demands.

"Angie, I did all those things because I didn't want you to become like me. I was a very talented nurse at your age, but I wasted it. And now here I am retiring from my job. But the truth is I actually retired years ago. I was already fully retired at age 35. What I'm trying to say is that I stopped giving my all in my job and started just going through the motions when I came to work."

Angie begins to listen intently.

"My boss back then tried to do to me what I was doing to you. Angie, when you have talent like you do, you must be hungry for more than food, and be thirsty for more than water. I counted all the times you said during evaluations that you felt overworked and underpaid. Well, guess what? Practically every nurse in the country feels that way. Be allergic to average. Do you remember when we had that blowup in the meeting and I asked you when you were going to start acting like a leader, and you said, when you pay me more? I didn't know whether to laugh or be disappointed."

Angie smiles and shakes her head.

"Angie, from this point forward," Susan tells her, "if you don't want to end up like me, then don't let your salary define your mentality."

Angie nods slightly in agreement.

"When you don't give your all, you pause your personal potential. In all my years as a nurse, I discovered that there are two types of nurses: professionals and amateurs. Amateurs come to work every day and on purpose they look for shortcuts. It's like their goal is to figure out how they can get paid the same amount of money for doing the least amount of work. When they are feeling good, they are great to work with and they deliver exceptional customer service to patients and co-workers, but when they aren't feeling good, for whatever reason, they are horrible to work with and will do just enough to get by. Professionals, on the other hand, are those nurses who consistently perform regardless of how they feel. Hours cut. Angry patients. Conflict with a co-worker. So what? They will still focus on positive results. Now that's hard to do, which is why every nurse is not a professional, even though they think they are."

They both laugh.

"Thank you," Angie tells Susan. "And I am sorry I was so rebellious."

"Oh, you don't have to apologize. And please don't do this for me, Angie. Don't do it for the company, don't do it for your new boss, don't do it for the patients. Do it for yourself."

Susan hands Angie the bottle of water again, and says, "Just like how water is essential to people and we can't live without it, be so good at what you do that people can't ignore you." Angie takes the bottle of water and opens it, just like she has opened her mind, and then drinks some, just like she was swallowing Susan's wisdom.

LEADERSHIP DROPS OF INSIGHT

- Amateurs only perform when they feel like it.

- Professionals perform regardless of their feelings.

CHAPTER 3:
UNFOLLOW THE LEADER

*People don't quit jobs. They quit a
boss, a supervisor, a manager, or
a hostile work environment.*

"They should be happy they have a job." Steve, a supervisor for a collections agency in Dallas, is explaining to his staff what Gina, the center manager, said about everyone having to work overtime and why she isn't hiring extra people to help with the workload.

As the group of employees socializes in the middle of the floor, someone whispers, "Here comes Sergeant Gina," sending the group scattering like roaches. Gina is walking the floor introducing a new employee named April. In her hand is the signature cup of ice that she chomps on throughout the day. As she walks April around, she points out her new colleagues. "That's Passive Aggressive Paul and Timid Tim. Over there is Burned Out Bob, Negative Nancy, and finally

Mediocre Mark."

"Hi, Sergeant Gina," replies Mark.

April, looking confused, says, "So everyone has a nickname?"

"Pretty much," says Gina. "And pretty soon you will as well."

Gina's cellphone rings. "I have a two o'clock call. Mark, finish introducing April to the team. I have to run."

As Mark continues to walk April around, introducing her to the team, she asks, "Okay, so can you tell me why everyone has these weird nicknames? Or is this a joke or what?"

"It's not a joke," says Mark. "Gina, or Sergeant Gina, gives everyone a nickname after your first 90 days of working here."

"And people are okay with her choices?"

"It's not that we're okay with it, we just have to accept it. That's how she is."

"Wow! I have never heard of anything this bizarre in the workplace before," says April.

"Gina has a long military background," Mark tells her, "and when she was hired about ten years ago, she hit the profit numbers upper management wanted and so they just kept her. The only thing they really care about is profits, not people."

"Yeah, but people drive profits," says April.

A month later, April is working at her desk when Sergeant Gina stops by and says, "I'll see you in my office in five minutes." April picks up a printout and heads to Gina's office. The door closes as multiple employees look on as if they know what is about to happen.

Chomp, chomp, chomp. Gina is chewing on crushed ice as usual. "So, what do you have for me April?" she asks as April hands her a one-page report.

"I know you are primarily concerned with the bottom line, so I put together some data on how to improve those numbers."

"Turnover, employee engagement, productivity lost, okay, all this data means nothing to me," says Gina.

"Well, it should!" replies April.

Gina looks up, shocked at April's tone and choice of words.

"What I mean is that these things all drive profitability. You see our turnover rate is 55 percent."

"Yes, I know what turnover is. It's a tough job, and people quit."

"Yeah, some people quit and leave, but some people have quit and stayed."

Gina looks up at April, as April focuses on the report.

"Look, let's get down to brass tacks," says Gina. "Are you telling me that this center is losing more than $2 million dollars annually because of turnover and employees not being babied?"

"If you want to put it in those exact terms, then, yes," says April.

"Do you know why I always eat ice cubes?" asks Gina.

"No, I don't," April replies.

"Because it reminds me to stay hard, since going soft is a habit. So, who the hell do you think you are coming into my center and telling me how to run it?" Gina shouts as she stands up out of her chair.

April is silent and holds up her hands, looking away.

"Get your ass out of my office and get back to work."

April is stunned. She stands up and says, "All of your employees are scared of you, Gina."

"So what? It builds character."

"I refuse to accept this type of behavior from a manager," April says as she walks to the door.

"You'll accept it if you want to keep your job!" yells Gina.

April turns back to look at Gina. "Have you ever heard of the EEOC?" she asks.

"Yep, it's against the law to discriminate against protected classes, but not against the law for me to make your life a living hell if I feel like it."

April shakes her head and says, "I quit."

"Oh, that's one I haven't heard before. See ya!" Gina says as she sits back down in her chair.

The rest of the staff who witnessed the scene are paralyzed, just blankly looking at both of them.

"All of you are fools if you continue to accept this!" April yells at them.

Today, you can still find Sergeant Gina running her center like a dictator. Turnover is still the same, and the employees are disengaged, but Gina still achieves her numbers using fear as her sole motivator, crushing morale just like she crushes ice.

LEADERSHIP DROPS OF INSIGHT

♦   If people follow you because they have to, you're a title leader.

♦   If people follow you because they want to, you're an authentic leader.

CHAPTER 4:
IT IS WHAT IT IS

*Accepting mediocrity or
expecting greatness?*

"It is what it is," says Tom in the managers' meeting for a state government agency.

"What exactly do you mean by that?" asks Terry, another manager.

"What I mean is that we have to understand that when working for the state, we have to hire whoever we can to fill the position. And let's be honest, we haven't been selecting the cream of the crop, but we have to do what we have to do to fill the position."

"So, what I'm hearing from you is that the reason we aren't exceeding expectations is because we can't hire the best people?"

"Like I said, it is what it is."

"I think what Tom is saying," adds another manager named Kelly, "is that we can't expect to go from good to great as an agency if we can't hire the best people. And in addition to that, we don't pay people that great, so they don't stay. Other offices also experience this kind of turnover, so it's not like we're the only ones."

Nods of agreement are displayed and heard by the majority of managers inside the small conference room.

Jon, a manager who is legally blind, shakes his head and starts laughing uncontrollably. All ten of the managers turn and look at him.

"Ha, ha, ha, I cannot believe what I'm hearing," says Jon, glancing at them as if he can see perfectly. "Listen to all of us. Are we serious? It is what it is, the other offices have turnover, and we're not the only ones. Are we really serious?" Jon stands up with his folded walking stick in hand. "You know there was a time in my career, years ago, when I could see. I have seen unmotivated employees who only show up for a paycheck. I have seen bully supervisors who are really just insecure. I have seen morale so low that employees had to pray together in order to stay together. But nothing and, dammit, I mean nothing, is like the sight of seeing a leadership spirit extinguished right before your eyes. What are we becoming, guys? We are a government agency, which means we have to keep adapting to change. Can we control the president and Congress about these new health care laws? Can we control the state government for requiring us to take over new systems, new policies, and procedures? Can we?"

"No," replies Tom.

"What can we control?" Jon says, pointing to his heart. "We can only control how we respond to our workplace situations and circumstances. It is what it is. I'm sorry, Tom, but that phrase is the motto of a stagnant mentality. When we say that, we stop thinking, we stop being innovative and creative, we stop searching for ideas. It is what it is, no, it is what we make it to be! Tom, it's hard to hear that coming from a man like you, who came up with the solution to redesign our client customer service program. When I hear us say that we aren't the only state office with high turnover, it makes me cringe, because it says we're accepting average. It says we're comfortable with the status quo. Dammit, let's not lower our expectations just to get a warm body in here, because that costs us more in the long run when you add up all the costs of posting the job, interviewing, and training. Guys, leadership is not just about hiring the person with the best resume, it's about hiring the best fit. And it's also about developing and growing the people that we already have. We have discounted our ability to influence as leaders. We want our employees to trust us, but we don't really trust them, and guess what, they know it. They can feel it. We have to be transparent with them, just like this bottled water." Jon grabs a bottle of water and holds it in the air.

"Jon, what you're saying sounds good, but how do we get employees to be accountable and stop making excuses?" asks Kelly. "I mean we can't teach that, so you gotta hire for that. I think that's what we are all saying."

"Kelly, are leaders born or made?" Jon asks.

"I would say made."

"And if they're made, do you need a title to be a leader?"

"Not necessarily."

"Then what makes them into leaders?"

"Experience."

"Right! And so as leaders we have to ask ourselves how we create the right experiences and environment for people to learn, develop, display, and repeat the desired behaviors we need in order to take our agency from good to great."

"Okay, Jon, so what does that look like, since you seem to have all the answers?" Tom asks somewhat sarcastically.

"It's being the change you want to see, Tom," answers Jon. "It's called contagious leadership, in which you infect your staff with energy and enthusiasm. It's also called leading by example, which may be common sense, but which we know is not common practice. It looks like this if your staff has accountability issues. Tom, the next time you make a mistake, call a team meeting for your entire staff."

"That's a lot of meetings, Jon," Tom says jokingly as the others laugh.

"And in that meeting, share with the team the mistake you made. Tell them you take full responsibility for it, no excuses, and then tell them how it will actually impact the team. Finally, tell them what you would do differently next time."

"So they can learn from it and not repeat it," says Kelly.

"Exactly," replies Jon.

"And also, if you do that, it may give them the courage to not make excuses the next time they make a mistake, because they see how you as a manager are always sharing your mistakes," adds Terry.

"Now you got it!" says Jon. "That's truly leading by example."

The managers nod in agreement, and whispers of support, positivity, and hope permeate the room. Jon unfolds his walking stick and strolls toward the first manager, extending and shaking his hand. He does this with everyone in the room and is the last person to leave and turn off the lights.

LEADERSHIP DROPS OF INSIGHT

- ♦ Be allergic to average.

- ♦ It is what you make it to be.

- ♦ Be the behavior you wish to see.

CHAPTER 5:
SEEDS OF GREATNESS

Leaders grow people.

As leaders, we are like farmers and our employees are like seeds. Seeds have everything they need inside of them to grow and achieve their highest potential, if, that is, they are in an environment that is conducive to their growth. As leaders, we are responsible for cultivating that environment.

You can take any seed of your choice—an apple seed or a pumpkin seed, for example—and those seeds will lay dormant for months or even years, until they feel the environment is just right for their growth. If a seed is not exposed to sufficient moisture, proper temperature, enough oxygen, and, for many seeds, light, the seed will not start the growth process.

Employees are just like seeds. If they are not exposed to a fertile foundation of trust, do not get sufficient amounts of respect and recognition shining down on them, and do not receive a proper flow of open communication, the employees will remain uninspired to excel, grow, and break out of their comfort zone, the employees may be idle and develop a paycheck mentality, or they may do just enough to get by.

HOW LEADERS GROW PEOPLE

Be helpful not hurtful

RESPECT

Offer praise and recognition

Focus on facts not feelings

OPEN COMMUNICATION

Encourage feedback and involve them

As leaders we are like farmers and our employees are like seeds. Seeds have everything they need inside them to grow and achieve their greatest potential if they are in an environment that facilitates their growth. As leaders we are responsible for cultivating that environment.

Be open-minded and listen

Do what you say

Admit mistakes

FOUNDATION OF TRUST

JAMES BIRD GUESS
INTERNATIONAL SUCCESS ACADEMY

CHAPTER 6:
THE COACH

Employee performance usually falls into three categories: the don't know hows, the can't dos, and the won't dos.

Sarah is working late again as usual. She typically stays after all of her employees have left for the day to complete her tasks and duties as supervisor. Her boss, Robin, is headed home and notices her still working.

"Sarah, how late are you going to be here tonight?" Robin asks.

"At least till 8."

"What about your son's play at the new art complex? I thought you were all excited about it."

"Yeah, my husband is going to take him. I just have so much I have to get done."

Lightning strikes and thunder announces the sudden rain outside.

"Look, I know how important family is to you," says

Robin. "Talk to me about what's going on every week that's causing you to work so much that you miss the most important things in life?"

"My people need me," says Sarah. "They struggle throughout the day, they always have questions and need me to help put out the fires, and this is the only time I don't get interrupted, so I have to stay late to make it all happen."

"Sarah, you've got to stop doing this."

"You mean stop helping my staff, making sure they don't fail? That's part of my job as supervisor, right?"

"Yes, it is part of your job to help them," asserts Robin, "but it appears that you're handicapping them. It seems like they're dependent on you for everything."

Sarah smiles sheepishly.

"Remember when you went on vacation to Miami last month and you couldn't even enjoy the trip because of the constant e-mails and text messages from your staff?"

"Is it really such a bad thing that they need me?" asks Sarah. "I'm trying to lead by example and be a team player. That's part of our company values."

"It's not that it's a bad thing that they need you, but it would be a great thing if they didn't."

Sarah's face wrinkles. Robin starts to explain her point. "Sarah, do you remember what happened to Joe Sax?"

"Of course. How could I forget?"

"As you know, Joe was remarkably talented. His skill set, education, certifications, I mean Joe excelled at everything technical related to his job. He was constantly promoted, up to the position of director, then his gift turned into a curse. Year after year started to pass him by and once he turned 50, the unwritten company rule that when you get to that age you start to clog the company's pipeline for talent development took effect, and his career stagnation began. Sarah, most managers are still unaware of the 'escalator formula' for professional success. Most of them are still trying to climb the corporate ladder."

"Okay, what exactly is the escalator formula?" a bewildered Sarah asks.

"The escalator formula is similar to the 80/20 rule, except it's 15/85, which means 15 percent of your professional success comes from just being exceptional at doing your job, while 85 percent of your professional success comes from your ability to effectively interact with and lead people."

Sarah is focused on every word that leaves her boss' mouth. Robin continues: "Some managers take pride in the fact that their employees cannot go a single day without relying on them. They feel indispensable and it boosts their self-esteem. But upper management in our organization actually perceives it as lackluster leadership and the inability to develop people and support succession planning. That's why so many managers and directors are stuck in the same positions with the same responsibilities for years and years, and they are eventually pushed out at a certain age because of the fear of infecting others and causing organizational stagnation."

Sarah looks stunned.

"I am giving you the rules to the game here that I am not supposed to share with you yet, but we need more women leaders in this company and I want you to have a head start."

"Thank you, Robin. You've always been there for me and supported me. What exactly do you suggest I do?"

"Coach your people and develop them so that they're not dependent on you. One of the ways you can do that is to stop giving them all the answers and putting out all of the fires. Who would you say interrupts you the most, or seems to always need the most help?"

"I would say Scott," Sarah tells her.

"Okay, from this point forward, when Scott comes to you for assistance, I want you to just ask him a series of questions. For example, ask him, What have you considered so far? Will that contribute to our goals and ultimate vision? What are the advantages and disadvantages of that action?"

"Yeah, but I know Scott, and he will get frustrated and just want me to give him the answer. Plus, doesn't it take a lot of time to get him to think it through, especially if he struggles? I mean, wouldn't it be easier to just give him the answer so we can both get back to work?"

Robin laughs. "Remember, the key is to develop your people, not handicap them. So, yes, in the beginning it will take some time and work to coach him, but that's part of the growth process. You don't see the flowers and trees outside complaining about the rain, do you? They understand that the rain is necessary for their growth. Be like rainwater, Sarah. Be essential to Scott's growth. Soon Scott will realize that if he comes to you, you are going to guide him to the solution rather than give him the solution, and you will have truly taught him to have a problem-solving mentality."

"Wow, I can't thank you enough for the advice, Robin."

"You're so welcome," Robin replies.

"Well, I think I am going to get out of here and go see my son in his play," Sarah says with confidence.

"Spoken like a true leader," says Robin.

LEADERSHIP DROPS OF INSIGHT

- When a professional athlete has a slump, his team doesn't trade him, they coach him. Approach your employees with the same mentality.

CHAPTER 7:
LEADING CHANGE

You cannot change people. You can only change how you respond to people, which may change how they respond to you.

Julie, who has grown up around the oil and gas industry her whole life, is a manager for an oil and gas company in Houston, Texas. Having just completed her master's degree, she obtained what she thought would be her dream job, but it's turning out to be her worst nightmare.

"Okay, gentlemen, I have some ideas about how to improve productivity in each of your respective areas," Julie says one day in her department meeting. All of the 20 men in the meeting are roughly twice her age. They look at her with their arms folded and their eyes filled with doubt, and the only sound is a silent room of disengagement. As she begins communicating her ideas using a PowerPoint slide demonstration, a colleague name John chimes in sarcastically: "We tried that before you were born." The entire room fills with laughter. Julie gives John a sarcastic smile and says, "Thanks, John. Now back to what I was saying." As Julie continues, one of the men gets up and leaves. A few minutes later, another man leaves, and then another. Julie continues to present her ideas until only a few men are left listening. "Is there something going on that I'm not aware of?" she asks, confused. The five men left in the room shrug their shoulders.

Julie goes back to her office and pops three aspirin for her pounding headache. Realizing the bottle is now empty, she rubs her forehead and tosses the aspirin bottle in the trash. With her door closed, the tears come and fall in a familiar place.

As she waits in the lunch line the next day, Julie is feeling frustrated and hopeless. A hundred thoughts go through her head. Why doesn't her team like her? Why don't they believe in her ideas? Why do they resist change?

"Next," says the cook as Julie approaches. "What will it be, miss?" he asks.

"I'll take the chef's salad with vinaigrette dressing."

"Okay, it will be a few minutes while I make the vinaigrette dressing."

"No problem, that's fine."

As Julie waits for her salad, she watches the chef prepare the dressing. The chef is singing while he works. "Oil and water, the perfect combination," he shouts.

"I love that dressing, it tastes so good," Julie says to him.

"You love the taste, and I love the process of making oil and water mix," the chef replies.

"Ha, ha, oil and water never mix. Trust me, I have been around the oil industry all my life."

"Then you never understood the myth of oil and water and how they are just like people," the chef insists. "You see, the first reason that water and oil don't mix is because they are fundamentally different. Just like all of us are different, whether it's age, beliefs, or personality. Water is naturally dense, and if we take equal parts of water and oil, there will still be more water than oil, which means that water will always sink underneath the oil. The other reason they cannot mix with each other is that water is positively charged and oil has no charge at all, so there is no force between the substances that allow them to mix. Just like how some people are optimists and always positive and some are pessimists and frequently negative. Therefore, even if you stir a container with oil and water, the two will eventually separate into two distinct layers since oil resists water, just like people resist change."

Julie listens and smiles. "Tell me about it," she replies.

"Ah, but most people aren't aware that there is one way that oil and water can mix."

"Do enlighten me," says Julie.

"I can show you better than I can tell you," says the

chef. "Watch this."

Julie watches the chef prepare the dressing. He mixes vinegar, then adds egg yolks and mustard (Julie cringes), and finally adds the oil slowly. "Wow," she says, "maybe I shouldn't have looked. I didn't know you added all that in the dressing."

"It's a process called emulsion," the chef responds. "To make oil and water, or in this case oil and vinegar, mix, you have to break one liquid into tiny particles and use an emulsifier to keep the two substances from not separating as quickly to maximize the flavor of the dressing. It's just like how with people we sometimes have to be emulsifiers, since people resist change like oil resists water. We have to do it slowly and then break down the change into small portions and add key people as emulsifiers to help keep the change intact and from separating again."

The chef then pours the fresh dressing onto Julie's plate of romaine. Julie smiles. "Thanks, chef. Have a great day!"

"And you as well," he replies.

Eating back in her office, Julie analyzes the salad dressing. "Oil and water don't mix, like people. With emulsifiers, oil and water can mix. Oil resists water, like people resist change," she thinks to herself. Paralyzed by thought and insight, she drops her fork and looks at the ceiling. "That's it!" she shouts.

Over the next week, she meets individually with four of the men on her team, who are all well respected by the entire office. She tells each of them that she knows they can probably do her job forwards and backwards, and says that she will do her best to make sure that if any promotional opportunities become available, that they are prepared for them.

"I am really going to need your help to take this team to the next level," she tells one of them during their meeting. "Phil, what are your thoughts on this?" she asks him. "You're finally learning," he remarks. "I just want my team to be successful," replies Julie.

During her next department meeting, Julie uses no PowerPoint slides and surprises her staff. Instead, she kicks off the meeting by engaging the team with questions. And she notices something remarkable. The men were more engaged than ever and contributed ideas once they saw some of the other men they respected contributing. Julie then collects, summarizes, and clarifies their ideas on one side of a whiteboard. On the other side she lists the following six questions: What is changing? Why is it changing? When is it changing? What are your roles? What does success look like? How are we capable of making the change successful?

"Phil, Bryan, Ed, and Joe, can you all help guide this discussion?" asks Julie.

The men know exactly what to do and have the team huddle into small groups to discuss their answers to the six questions.

"So, what the hell we are doing is we are changing how we are going to respond," John says with a smile, and the entire team laughs. Julie looks around and can't believe what she's witnessing—cooperation and buy-in.

She immediately thinks back to the oil and water. "I was the water and the team was the oil," she says to herself. "Emulsifiers," she mumbles, hearing the chef's voice in her head. "Phil, Bryan, Ed, and Joe are the emulsifiers. Break the substance down into small parts and slowly and gradually add the oil into the mixture."

A week later, Julie is standing in the lunch line waiting to order another salad.

"Where's the chef today?" Julie asks one of the employees.

"Here he comes," the man replies. But it's not the same chef as before.

"Is the chef from last week off today or on vacation?" she asks.

"No, he quit," the new chef answers.

Julie has a look of shock and disappointment.

"No worries, sweetheart," says the new chef, "because I am one of the best!"

Julie looks at him as he pours a bottle of vinaigrette into a bowl. "You're not making the vinaigrette from scratch?" she asks.

"Ha, nobody does that anymore. There's no time, plus it's too hard to make the water and oil mix. You need a machine for that."

"Thanks," Julie says to him as she walks out of the line.

LEADERSHIP DROPS OF INSIGHT

- ◆ People don't destroy that which they help create.

- ◆ Double your question-to-statement ratio. Ask more questions to involve others and allow them to contribute to ideas to achieve cooperation and buy-in.

CHAPTER 8:
THE COPY AND PASTE LEADER

Never become too busy to lead.

Jack is the executive director of a nonprofit organization that provides services for people struggling with substance abuse and mental challenges. After being notified of an employee complaint from the corporate office hotline, he was told to provide training for all employees on sensitivity, diversity, and team building.

Jack calls Paul, a colleague who is a well-known management consultant. "Hi, Paul," he says. "I know it's been a while, but I was wondering if you had a training program on sensitivity and team building?"

"Sure," Paul replies. "Are you certain that's exactly what you need?"

"Yeah, corporate wants us to do it," Jack tells him.

Later, Jack and Paul meet in person to go over the outline and goals of the training program.

"Jack, before I deliver any training program, I

always like to know a few important things to help make the training successful," Paul says.

"Absolutely. Shoot!" Jack answers.

"What is the vision for the organization?"

Jack pauses and then glances at a picture on the wall. Paul notices the picture as well.

"We help those who are ..."

Paul interrupts Jack before he can finish. "Now I know you all have a mission statement, but what I am curious about is where the organization is going in the next five to seven years. In other words, what are you and your team striving and stretching to become?" he asks.

"Right. Do we really need that in order to do the training?" Jack asks, looking confused.

"Well, I just want you to understand that to make the training sustainable and to maximize the return on your investment, your employees need to know and understand the ultimate vision and direction. Jack, I want you to understand that as a fairly new and young executive director, your number one job is probably one that's not even listed in your job description, and that is to cultivate an environment of confidence in the future. Also, it's going to be very important that you make this initiative top of your agenda, so that everyone understands the importance of it. They should hear you refer to it constantly, in meetings, one-on-ones, and especially during performance evaluations."

Jack breathes a long sigh. "Paul, I hear you. This

just sounds like it's going to be a lot of busy work."

"Authentic leadership requires effort, but so does growth of teams," Paul responds.

The following week, Jack and Paul are meeting again to discuss the plan for implementing the training in phases, starting with the senior leadership team. "Okay, so I went online and Googled a few vision statements that I like from some similar organizations and sort of merged them all into one short and meaningful sentence like you mentioned," Jack tells Paul. "Also, I found a pretty good team values agreement and I thought it would be nice to have each staff member read it and then sign it so they will be committed to it. It says a lot about respect for each other, teamwork, and other things related to sensitivity and being a team player."

Paul cringes as Jack unveils his plagiarized copies of a vision statement and team values agreement. As Paul shakes his head, Jack pauses with frustration.

"Jack," Paul interjects, "I know your intentions are good, but we will fail miserably if we just copy vision statements from other organizations and then attempt to paste them into one for our own organization. Recently, I was coaching an executive with a Fortune 500 corporation who was struggling to effectively lead his people. We discovered his biggest obstacle was credibility and authenticity."

Jack listens attentively as Paul continues. "You see, he would constantly read what I call the 'leadership du jour,' or the latest and greatest best-selling books on leadership. Now, of course, I strongly believe in being a lifelong learner, but this executive would always try to copy and paste the latest leadership best practices and philosophy into his company. And his employees simply rolled their eyes every other year as he announced a bold new vision or some innovative change. He lost credibility long ago and was suffering from leadership delusion, and I don't want that to happen to you, Jack. Make sense?"

"Yeah, makes a lot of sense," Jack responds. "But Paul, you know I don't really need all this vision stuff, I mean …"

Paul interrupts him again, immediately interjecting, "But your employees need it."

"I know you're right, Paul. I just feel like all of this keeps me from doing my real work."

"What do you consider your real work?" Paul asks him.

"Funding strategies, and making sure everyone is performing the necessary tasks and duties."

Paul responds quickly, explaining, "Jack, many people can manage, but only a few people can lead. As executive director, your real work is people. Not tasks, not strategies, not reports, but people. People will drive every number and key performance metric, and your people will also determine whether any organizational strategy succeeds or fails. Jack, what I am trying to tell you is that a vision statement can't come from a Google search. It has to come from a search of your heart. If it comes from your heart, you will believe it. If you believe it, you will act it. And when you act it, your employees will feel it and you will deposit authenticity into their minds and heart."

Jack nods in agreement. "I've got a lot of homework to do," he tells Paul.

"Yes sir, you do, and as your coach, I will help you," says Paul.

"So I guess we should scrap having the employees sign the team agreement as well, right?" Jack asks.

"If we just have them read it and sign it, what do you think will happen?"

"Well, I was hoping we could have something for them to take ownership of and also hold them accountable to."

"Yes, but what could probably happen three months after they all read it and sign it?" Paul asks.

"They don't actually do it," responds Jack.

"And do you understand why they probably won't do it?"

"Because they just didn't believe any of it, I guess."

"Yes, but also because they didn't come up with it or have any input in it. It can't truly be the team's values if the executive director comes up with them on his own. The employees will just feel like they are being forced to do it, instead of wanting to do it. People tend not to destroy that which they help to create, right?"

"Yep, you're right. That makes sense."

Over the next three months, Paul starts to deliver the training to the senior-level leaders and then to the mid-level managers. He has weekly coaching discussions with Jack as well. After the last training session, Paul and Jack talk one last time.

"Wow, it's been great," says Jack. "I know the staff loved the process and are already starting to apply some of it."

"That's awesome!" says Paul. "Jack, I just want to reemphasize to you that this entire initiative and whether or not it will fail or succeed will be due to us. I will take it personally if we fail, and I hope you will as well. To me, that's a big part of leadership."

"I definitely agree. We have to keep the momentum going, and I have to be the motivation for the team."

Six months later, unfortunately Jack has fallen back into his comfort zone of managing tasks and being too busy to lead. Another employee has called the corporate office hotline and Jack is being heavily scrutinized by his boss.

LEADERSHIP DROPS OF INSIGHT

♦ What you want is a ropes course for your team, but what your team needs is for the senior leaders to lead by example.

♦ The manager says dealing with people issues takes too much time away from my real work. The leader says my people are my real work.

CHAPTER 9:
BREAK THE GOLDEN RULE

You shouldn't treat everyone the same,
but you should treat everyone fairly.

Applause fills the conference room. "Great job, Mary," says Sandra, a manager for a nationwide retail store, as she asks the team to recognize Mary, who has just completed a major project for the company way ahead of the deadline. Mary, standing up, appears reserved, embarrassed, and somewhat nervous. Still, she smiles through it.

Three months later, Sandra is having her routine biweekly department meeting in a large conference room with 35 of her staff members. "Charles, since last November, we keep missing the mark," she says excitedly. "This performance sucks, and is not what we are known for. When I was managing that piece of business five years ago, we never dropped below 50 percent. Let's go, man. It's like the fourth quarter and two-minute warning time!" Charles nods in agreement.

It's 7 p.m., and the cleaning crew has just arrived as Sandra is working in her office, loud music blasting from her computer speakers. She gets up to approach the woman vacuuming outside her office. "Excuse me, do you speak English?" she asks. The woman turns off the vacuum, smiles, shakes her head, and says no in an apologizing tone. "You should really learn English," Sandra tells her. "It might make your job easier, and there are free classes on YouTube now." The woman nods, but doesn't understand a word. Sandra heads to restroom.

As she is walking back to her office, a man approaches her. "Excuse me, my name is Juan. Did you need anything?"

"Hi, Juan. Nope, I'm good."

"Okay, my sister said she thought you needed something, so I was just checking."

"Ah, so you must be the head honcho and owner of the cleaning business, huh?"

Juan smiles at her. "Yes, it's a family owned business."

"I was just telling your sister she might want to learn English since she's in America now. I mean, if I was her, I would try to learn English immediately so I could better communicate with people."

"Oh, okay. Thanks, we will keep that in mind."

"Look, don't take any offense," Sandra tells him. "I'm just trying to help you guys."

"You guys?" Juan asks, feeling offended.

"Look, Jose ..."

"Juan. My name is Juan."

"I mean, Juan. I am not trying to sound racist or anything. Again, I am just trying to be helpful. I always treat people the way I want to be treated."

Juan, in a passive aggressive tone, responds, "Maybe that's the problem. Try thinking about how others would like to be treated rather than how you would like to be treated." Juan turns on his sister's vacuum and walks away. Sandra wrinkles her face and thinks to herself, "People are so sensitive."

The next day, Sandra is still thinking about the incident with Juan. His voice and words remain stuck in her head: "Try thinking about how others would like to be treated rather than how you would like to be treated."

At one point, Tom, another manager, peeks in and asks, "Hey, Sandra, are we still on for lunch at 11:30?"

"Yes, sir, we are. Hey Tom, you got a minute?"

"Sure. What's up?"

Sandra closes the door to her office. "Do I treat people how they would like to be treated?"

Tom laughs hysterically.

"What?" Sandra asks.

"Is this some type of joke?" Tom asks, still laughing.

"Tom, I'm serious."

"Okay, do you want the truth?"

"Yes, of course I do," Sandra answers.

"You can't handle the truth," Tom says jokingly.

"Tom, I am serious. I need your honest opinion, please."

Realizing that Sandra is serious, Tom responds, "No, you don't, Sandra. But that's just your management and personality style."

Sandra leans back in her chair and sighs.

"Why are you so concerned about other people's feelings all of sudden?" Tom asks.

"What do you mean all of sudden? I care about my people," Sandra responds.

"Well, I'm not saying that you don't care. I'm just saying I've never seen you show it or be concerned like you are now."

"Okay, now you're criticizing me," Sandra says, laughing.

"No, I'm serious. I mean, remember that time when Mary completed that project way ahead of schedule and you made her stand up and be recognized by the entire department?"

"Yeah."

"Well, she was so embarrassed and nervous, her palms were drenched."

"Yeah, but everyone loves to be recognized. I just wanted to show her that we appreciate her. Plus, you know that management cliché, praise in public and criticize in private, right?"

"Not always true, Sandra," Tom admonishes. "Mary would have probably preferred that you praise and recognize her in your one-on-one sessions."

"You really think she didn't enjoy the attention? I mean I would have." Realizing what she just said, Sandra pauses, as Tom shakes his head to confirm what they both already know.

"Okay, I would love to coach you some more about your management and personality style, but anything else I will have to bill you for," says Tom.

"Thanks, Tom," Sandra replies. "See you at 11:30."

Throughout the day, Sandra begins to think about her behavior and treatment of several employees over the past few weeks. She says to herself: "No wonder Mary has not completed anything before the deadline or gone above and beyond recently. She is probably scared to death that I will humiliate her in public again. I love public recognition, but she doesn't. And Charles, poor Charles, the guy just stuck his tail between his legs when I challenged him in front of the team. Had that been me, I would have accepted the challenge and proved my worth. Ugh! I have been demotivating my people, and here I am thinking I am motivating them. I've got to get better as a manager."

Over the next six months, Sandra makes a deliberate effort to not treat people how she would like to be treated, but rather how they would like to be treated. And, of course, she does it with her usual electric personality.

LEADERSHIP DROPS OF INSIGHT

♦ All of your employees are different and they all need different things to maximize their engagement. Identify what's important to them, know how they like to communicate, how they like to be recognized, and how they accept feedback, and adapt to them instead of expecting them to adapt to you. Serve your people.

CHAPTER 10:
THE POWER OF ADAPTABILITY

It is not the most educated leader, the most experienced, or the most intelligent who will be successful in today's workplace. It is the one who can best adapt to different people, situations, and circumstances.

The average leader can generally lead people who look like them, are the same ethnicity, have a similar educational background, are around the same age, and have the same religious beliefs, but it takes an adaptable leader to lead people who are completely different than they are. These differences often cause conflict and cause others to make judgments, labeling others who are different as right or wrong, or good and bad.

Changing Chameleons

The power of adaptability is a skill or quality that

can be learned. Examples of the quality can be seen throughout nature. Like the chameleon. In order to survive, the chameleon will change the color of its skin to adapt to its environment and camouflage itself. The chameleon truly understands that it cannot change its environment or the situations and circumstances surrounding it, and that the only thing it can change is how it responds to its environment.

Palm Tree People

During a hurricane, hundreds of trees are broken and destroyed. The oak tree is a very strong tree with bark and strong roots. However, the oak tree is no match for a strong hurricane. Because the oak tree is so rigid, it tends to break when encountering strong winds and storms.

The palm tree is very different than the oak tree, especially during storms like a hurricane. Even during strong storms like Hurricane Andrew and Hurricane Katrina, the palm tree can survive because of its ability to adapt. Unlike the oak tree that attempts to fight the wind and water with strength, the palm tree bends with the wind. The palm tree will bend all the way to the ground to weather the storm. As leaders of people, we must also bend with the winds of change and conflict to avoid breaking.

The Growth Process

The human body contains roughly 640 muscles. In order to maintain a healthy body, it is very important to exercise those muscles. People spend countless hours attempting to make their muscles grow. Muscles are remarkable in that they also have the natural ability to adapt. However, the only time a muscle will grow is when it is knocked out of its comfort zone. When it encounters pressure and stress that it has never seen before, only then will the muscle start the process of growth.

The Seasons of Change

So many people quit in life. They quit their goals and place their greatest dreams on the shelf of mediocrity and just start going through the motions in life. There are four seasons in your professional life as well as your personal life. Just like the four seasons outside: summer, fall, winter, and spring. Your seasons as a leader in your professional and personal life are called summer success, fall failure, weary winter, and spectacular spring. This is why you must learn to adapt. Every three months, there will be peaks and valleys, ups and downs, highs and lows that you must adapt to. So many people quit in the middle of their season.

If things in your professional or personal life have been going great, get ready, because your season is about to change. If things have been going horribly in your life, then you must also get ready, because your season is about to change.

Water

Finally, water is another example of adaptability.

Wherever water goes, it adapts to its environment. When it's cold, water becomes ice. When it's warm, water becomes soft and flows. And when it's extremely hot, water can become a gas if necessary. Water will go around, over, or through any obstacles that stand in its way. Water matches the shape of any container. Water cannot be broken and is able to adapt to pressure and work around it.

LEADERSHIP DROPS OF INSIGHT

- Adapt or become obsolete, adapt or perish.

- Start doing things that make you uncomfortable. Like a muscle, periodically encounter and embrace pressure to start the growth process.

CHAPTER 11:
THE ROLY-POLY MANAGER

*Roly-polies are insects that got their name
because they can roll up into a ball to
avoid direct confrontation and protect
themselves from any perceived predators.*

Amanda just became the new superintendent for a small school district in Kansas. Sitting in her office, she is about to send out an e-mail addressing a certain issue. She reads her e-mail twice, tweaking it before sending it out to the entire staff. "And send," she says to herself.

Later that afternoon, in a meeting with her direct reports, she revisits the issue. "Please remember that we must all be on time to do our jobs. The taxpayers in our community are counting on us." Her staff looks at each other. After the meeting, a few staff members discuss what happened.

"You do know who she was talking about, right?"

Todd asks.

"Of course. Michelle is the only one who constantly comes in late," replies Abdul.

"Yep, but what gets me is why she treats all of us like we're the ones doing it, instead of just addressing Michelle directly."

"Because she's probably scared of Michelle. You do remember how Michelle blew up in the district meeting?"

"Yeah, that makes sense."

"Don't worry, with that type of leadership style, the board is going to eat her alive in the next few years. Amanda won't last two years. I give her three years max."

Amanda's contract was not renewed as superintendent, and she now works for another school in Pennsylvania, where she still displays passive aggressive behavior.

LEADERSHIP DROPS OF INSIGHT

- Water is clear and transparent.

- Mediocre managers are afraid to address a problem with a specific employee, so they send out an e-mail or in a meeting they generalize it and inform all employees to stop doing it. Each time you do that, you lose credibility as a leader.

CHAPTER 12:
PAYCHECK MENTALITIES

*You can pay for an employee's presence,
but you cannot pay for their heart.*

Mike, who works in a bank in central Illinois, is considered a "paycheck employee." When family and friends ask him about his work and if he enjoys it, he replies, "It's just a job. It pays the bills." His only reason for going to work is to receive a paycheck. Mike is not fully committed or uncommitted to his daily work, manager, or teammates. Instead, he performs just enough to get by. Often, he goes through the motions with tasks and duties and does not see any connection between his personal and professional goals and his job duties and responsibilities.

"Mike, we've got to talk about your attitude," Mike's manager, Ryan, says to him in a one-on-one meeting one day.

"What's wrong with my attitude?" Mike asks.

"Well, first of all, you're always late to work, you're always late to meetings, and your laziness is really starting to impact the rest of the team. Plus, I just don't see you taking ownership of your work."

Mike immediately becomes defensive. "Always late to work and always late to meetings? I was on time today and yesterday, so I don't understand ..."

Ryan interrupts him. "Mike, you know what I'm talking about."

Mike sighs and mumbles under his breath.

"Excuse me, did you want to say something?" Ryan asks.

"Yeah, I said you seem to always single me out, but you never say anything to Patricia and Thomas," Mike replies.

"Patricia and Thomas are performing well above average, and besides, this is not about them, this is about you."

"So is this meeting about my performance or my attitude?"

"Both! And look, I am not going to argue with you about this. Just be accountable and improve your attitude like an adult."

Mike sits in silence.

"Mike, do we understand each other?" Ryan asks.

"Yeah, I understand," Mike answers.

———————

It's one year later, and Mike is still working the same

job, with the same paycheck mentality. His former boss, Ryan, has since left the company, and Mike now reports to a woman named Cheryl. Cheryl is going through her first round of performance evaluations and Mike is next up on the list.

"Hi, Mike. How are you?" asks Cheryl.

"Good," Mike responds as they both sit down in an empty conference room.

Cheryl sits directly beside Mike. "Mike, I want to hold off on your performance evaluation and discuss something else in this meeting."

"Okay, what are we discussing?" he asks curiously.

"Mike, I noticed you were late to work on Monday, Tuesday, and Wednesday of last week, and also late to work and to three very important meetings this week. Mike, it seems like there is a lack of commitment on your part and I want to share with you how it's impacting the rest of the team."

Mike again immediately becomes defensive. "But I am not always late," he responds.

"Oh, no, I didn't say always late. But you do agree you were late to work on Monday, Tuesday, and Wednesday of last week, and also late to work and to three very important meetings on Monday and Tuesday of this week, right?"

"Yes, that's correct," Mike answers. "But ..."

Cheryl cuts him off. "Mike, let me just share with you how this impacts the team, and then I will definitely listen to you with my undivided attention."

Mike feels differently this time. He notices that

Cheryl is not attacking him, but is actually trying to make him feel comfortable.

"Mike, when anyone who does your job is late to work, it creates so much more work for your teammates. Think about Bob, Eddie, Tyler, and Joan, all of whom have to pull double duty, which means they're unable to give the customers their full attention, and, of course, we're all about ..." Cheryl pauses and waits for Mike to finish her sentence.

"The customer experience," Mike answers.

"Now, in addition to that, what message does it send to the rest of the team when you're late to our daily customer focus meetings, where we share stories of what exceptional customer service looks like?"

Mike pauses and thinks for a moment. "It probably sends a message that I don't care. But I actually do care."

"Mike, I know you care, but it's not so much about what you think or feel. It's about what I and your teammates actually see. Perception is ..."

"Reality," both she and Mike say at the same time. "Mike, come with me for a second," she continues.

Cheryl stands up and heads to the whiteboard. She begins to draw a circle with small squares inside it and starts to label them. Mike looks at her with a curious expression.

"Okay, so this circle represents the entire bank. And these smaller squares are the various departments within the bank. Mike, I want you to understand that you don't just process deposits, withdraws, and financial reports. What you do impacts this department"—she draws a line to another square—"and this department, which then impacts this department, which impacts our customers and their families and then comes all the way back to support you and your paycheck, and ultimately your family. Mike, I just want you to understand where you fit into the big picture of things."

Mike is in awe of her example of "the big picture," which Cheryl writes at the top of diagram.

"Huh, no one has ever really explained it to me like that before," says Mike.

"Mike, I've been in banking for more than 20 years, and the people I have seen become successful have specific qualities, and some of those qualities you already have. Now, I don't know what your ultimate career aspirations are, but I would like to know, so I can see how to help you achieve your goals, even if it's not in banking." A sudden rush of both excitement and hesitation overcomes Mike as he and Cheryl sit down for more than an hour, discussing goals and growth.

After that, Mike was still late to work and meetings from time to time, but every time he was, Cheryl simply reminded him of his potential and his goals. He was eventually promoted and replaced Cheryl as manager, after Cheryl was promoted to director.

The Puzzle of Purpose
Are you a leader attempting to communicate purpose to your people? Think of a puzzle inside a box. A

puzzle is made up of many pieces. The picture of what the puzzle is supposed to look like once it's completed is shown on the outside of the box. This "big picture" is like the vision for your organization, and the puzzle pieces represent the many tasks, goals, and responsibilities required to achieve the vision or big picture.

Just imagine if you gave a team of people different amounts of puzzle pieces and told them to put the puzzle together by a deadline, and yet you never showed them the big picture on the box. They would still probably be able to complete the puzzle, but they would be able to do it much faster and with less frustration if they knew the purpose, the vision, the big picture of what it's supposed to look like after all the hard work. Your job as an authentic leader is to keep showing them, keep reminding them in your own unique way, what the vision and big picture will look like once completed.

LEADERSHIP DROPS OF INSIGHT

- Water is essential. Be essential to people by identifying the most important things in life to them and helping them connect to a purpose. If employees are not connected to a purpose, they will focus on a paycheck.

- You can obtain what you want from others if you're willing to help others get what they want.

- When delivering criticism and feedback, criticize behavior, not personality. Focus on facts, not feelings. Be helpful, not hurtful.

CHAPTER 13:
THE LEADERSHIP HALO EFFECT

The leadership halo effect emerges when an overall impression of a manager or leader influences how people feel and think about his or her specific actions or behaviors.

Becky is the CEO of a large medical center and six months ago she hired Cindy as CFO to lead the business office.

"Becky, do you have a minute?" asks an employee named Linda one day.

"Sure. How are you?" Becky says with a smile, as Linda closes the door to her office.

"Not too good. I just wanted to say that I'm sorry, but I am handing in my resignation today."

"Wait, where is this coming from?" Becky asks, shocked.

"It's Cindy. I just can't work with her. Really, none of us can. Ever since she came onboard, it's been horrible."

Becky listens attentively, but ultimately she's unable to convince Linda to stay. They hug each other and say their good-byes.

Two weeks later, there is a knock on Becky's door. "Yes, come in," Becky says as she presses send on an e-mail. The door opens wide as ten ladies enter her office and close the door behind them. Becky looks anxious. "Hi, ladies. To what do I owe the pleasure of this visit?" she asks sheepishly. "Is there a birthday or something that I missed?"

"Becky, we all decided to come to you as a team because we respect and like you, but we just can't work for Cindy," an employee named Sarah tells her. The room fills with nods and echoes of "We just can't," and the employees begin to fill Becky in on some of their issues with Cindy.

"I understand," she tells them. "And I must say I am sorry, but I didn't realize things were this bad, and I'm going to address the issue with her today." Becky pleas for their patience. "You ladies know that I care about all of you and this hospital needs you, and I need you, so please just give me some time to work this out and I promise we will make this right."

The next day, a meeting occurs between Becky and Cindy. "Cindy," Becky begins, "I need you to understand that 95 percent of your team was ready to resign yesterday due to your leadership and communication style."

"What are they whining about now?" Cindy asks.

"Cindy, they are not whining. They are simply asking for effective leadership," Becky says as she hands Cindy a copy of a 360 evaluation summary that was completed for all of the hospital leaders two weeks ago. "The things I kept hearing over and over were micromanaging, lack of communication, keeps office door closed, and doesn't value our input." Becky points out to Cindy the highlighted summary of her evaluation and then asks her to come up with some ways to fix the issues. "I would like you to develop an action plan for how you can serve and lead your people moving forward based on the issues in the evaluation," she tells Cindy. "Come to my office first thing tomorrow morning and we'll discuss it. I have to leave now for a board meeting."

Later that night, Becky is reading the results of her own 360 evaluation from the entire office. She is surprised as she reads the feedback: "We love Becky," but Cindy is making her look bad at no fault of her own, even though she hired her. Cindy probably acted totally different during the interview process, like so many people do, because Becky would not have hired a person that is that deficient in people skills." She continues reading, thinking to herself, "They actually forgave me and still think of me in a positive light. Wow!"

The next morning, Becky is in her office early, checking e-mails and listening to voice mails, anxiously awaiting her meeting with Cindy. At 10 a.m., there's still no word from Cindy, who typically arrives at around 8. Becky goes to the break room for a can of Coke. She asks her administrative assistant, Glenda, if Cindy has made it in yet, since Cindy's door is closed. "She's been here since 8," Glenda responds in a soft tone. Becky goes back to her office.

At 5:30, Becky is just getting back from talking to a patient and her chief nursing officer. She sees that Cindy is working in her office with her headphones on. She waves at Cindy to get her attention, and Cindy removes her headphones.

"We were supposed to meet first thing this morning about your action plan," says Becky. "What happened?"

"Well, I thought about it last night, and I would like for you to just mentor me," Cindy replies.

Becky closes Cindy's door. "Cindy, please listen to me," she says firmly. "It's Friday and I am giving you two options. You can either come up with a development plan by Monday or else resign." Silence fills the room as they both look at each other.

Before leaving for the day, Becky contacts the human resource director at the corporate office to discuss possible termination options.

When Monday morning comes, Becky arrives at her usual time of 7 a.m. She has already finished her second can of Coke as she responds to e-mails and voice mails.

At 9 a.m., Becky is returning from walking the floor, talking with staff and patients. She glances at Cindy's office. Cindy's door is open, but she's not there. Becky asks Glenda if she's seen Cindy. "I think she went to grab some coffee," Glenda replies.

At 4 p.m., there's still no sign of Cindy. Becky prepares for "termination day."

The next morning, Becky walks into Cindy's office and asks her to go to the conference room with her. Cindy sees a human resources representative from corporate as she sits down. Becky closes the door. Becky begins to speak, but before one word can even leave her mouth, Cindy's eyes well up and she puts her hand in Becky's face and yells, "You're doing this right before Christmas!"

Becky and the human resources representative glance at each other. "Cindy, we talked about this and I gave you multiple chances to correct the situation," says Becky. Becky explains to Cindy how she is still going to give her full benefits, and details the other components of her severance package.

Two weeks later, an employee from the business office knocks on Becky's door. Becky, feeling anxious, stands up immediately and invites her in. "Hi, Sarah!" she says.

"Hi, Becky. I don't mean to bother you. I just wanted to say thank you. The business office feels so relieved with Cindy gone and you running the show for now. We understand you can't do it forever, but things are so much better."

"Well, we want to make sure the team has effective leadership in place to create an environment where you all can do your best work, and that's my job."

"Well, as a team, we will always speak up if we feel

something is not right."

Becky and Sarah hug each other and Sarah leaves.

As Becky closes her door, she sits down to reflect on what Sarah said, and she thinks about everything that has transpired over the last month. "I know they forgave me based on their feedback in the evaluations, but I am scared that they recognize how powerful they are and can use that over me in the future," Becky thinks to herself. "Where did I go wrong hiring Cindy? I should have asked more about her leadership and people skills. I was blinded by all of her technical skills. She was a CPA, and she had hospital experience, but I did not do enough due diligence on her people skills. But despite everything, the staff forgave me. Why, though? Because they like me, and because I always listen to them. But that doesn't mean they will forgive if I make another bad hiring decision. I wonder how many 'poor leadership credits' I have left with them."

LEADERSHIP DROPS OF INSIGHT

♦ Water is gentle, yet persistent.

♦ Every day you are either depositing trust or withdrawing trust from your leadership account. Many managers have insufficient funds.

ABOUT THE AUTHOR

Homeless after high school, James Bird Guess built a quarter-million-dollar business from the trunk of his car, and is now a renowned consultant and keynote speaker. His unique business acumen has led him to serve as a board member for the Salvation Army and Big Thought Inc.

A leading consultant to Fortune 500 and Fortune 1000 companies such as QuikTrip, United Surgical Partners International, and National Oilwell Varco, Guess currently serves as president of the International Success Academy, a management training and research company that facilitates leadership development, organizational culture change, staff retention strategies, and diversity and inclusion programs, and advises senior-level leaders on how to maximize organizational and employee performance.

Guess' leadership expertise in the health care, government, retail, education, nonprofit, and energy industries has helped him develop a unique background and insight to provide various perspectives for company leaders to make decisions that positively impact profitability, shareholder value, and employee engagement.

Made in the USA
Lexington, KY
11 October 2014